LETTERS TO PRINCE PAUL

LETTERS TO PRINCE PAUL

Volume 1

Foundations for your Life in Christ

Unless a grain of wheat fall
to the earth and dies . . . John 12:24

DAVID KOLB

To order additional copies of this book, contact:
Xlibris Corporation
1-888-795-4274
www.Xlibris.com
Orders@Xlibris.com
108338

Contents

Dedication and Thanks

This book is dedicated to all those saints who have walked in obedience to God and have done what is right even when it was unpopular and costly.

Thanks to Jud Quinelly who bribed me with a home cooked meal to get me to church where I came to Christ.

Thanks to Mama Singleton who always had ham soup cooking and an open house, and who said, "You can suggest anything to David. You just can't tell him anything."

Thanks to Rev. Dick and Patti Wiens for 17 years of guidance and for taking a chance on me and launching me into the ministry.

Thanks to my wife Joni, who is the epitome of perseverance, love and obedience. She has lived through adversity and forged on like no one I know.

Thanks to Joe and Kim Vogel for being obedient disciples of Christ and proving these thruths in daily life.

Thanks to Rosemary Manley for wading through my spelling and grammar.

Thanks to Jesus who holds the world together and ordains our footsteps.

Introduction

"Letters To Prince Paul" is a series of letters written to Prince Paul Konu, a church planter in Ghana West Africa. Prince Paul derives his title of prince from being son of a Ghana tribal chieftain of Ghana West Africa, even though Ghana has been a democracy for some time. In reality Prince Paul is a slave, a minister and bond-servant of the Lord Jesus Christ.

I met Prince Paul at a church leadership summit. Prince Paul and I were among about 16 pastors attending a basic discipleship-training group at the week long summit. By the end of the first day, the only people left in this group were Prince Paul, the facilitator and myself. Our facilitator asked us if we would like to cancel the session and we both said, "No!" Prince Paul needed to learn these things for the benefit of a rapidly developing movement of churches in Ghana, and I believe you can never review the basics enough. As a result the three of us spent the rest of the week discussing how to establish new believers in the gospel. Paul and I ate lunch and supper together each day, and prayed for each other, growing closer each moment. By the end of the week our hearts were knit much like David and Jonathan.

Though we are continents apart we have kept in touch with each other through the use of the Internet. During the following years I tried to get permission to forward various groups' Bible study materials to Prince Paul to use among his churches, but ran into a problem of "intellectual rights" costs. Individuals and publishers would ask for considerable sums of money to use their materials. These sums were far out of reach of this missionary, and would have been astronomical for Prince Paul. The average income in Ghana is about $25 per month and to the cost of printing materials is similar to those in the United States. Living "in culture" in Mexico on a subsistence income for more than a decade we fortunately understood the financial struggles of indigenous churches. As a result I asked permission from my mission to focus on writing leadership materials for Prince Paul.

The resulting first volume is what you see before you. Subsequent volumes are planned. We will be developing an Internet site in which leaders from developing nations can download these letters and use them in their ministries. They will also soon be translated into Spanish and made available to the entire Spanish Speaking world. Each volume is written to try to be universally culturally applicable.

If you are interested in using any of this information just contact us through our our web and license can be garnered for permission to copy all or part of this material as long as they do not do so for profit. The wisdom that God has given us is free. It is my philosophy that no one should be precluded from receiving it. My desire is that this is of great blessing to anyone who reads the pages that follow and that this and subsequent letters be of edification to the churches in the Kingdom of God worldwide.

From One Servant to Many Others,
Pastor Dave Kolb

First Letter to Prince Paul

Discipleship: Becoming God's Man

Hi Prince Paul,

I am glad that you like the idea of me writing letters to you for the project of spiritual growth that Partners In Christ has approved for me to do. In these letters I will address you as a learner at times and at other times as a peer. I know that you will be happy in whichever way I am speaking.

Feel free to share these with the men who are working in the village churches. These letters are written to them as well as to you. I am also sending them to some former disciples and friends to review and give feedback. Joni also reads them and makes comments on my writing style and how things are said. You will receive the original letters. The books that we put together will be somewhat different. I will not name you personally in my book unless you care to be mentioned.

The following is the first introductory letter:

Dear Prince Paul,

I hope that this letter finds you walking faithfully in the joy of the Lord while also enduring any hardship, which the Lord has sovereignly placed in your life.

With this letter and your permission I am going to begin to write to you as a disciple. To me, a disciple means many things, but most importantly it means that I look at you as a father looks at a son.

The goal of fatherhood is to bring a son to maturity so that the
young man walks in integrity, chooses to consult God and please Him
in all he does, sublimates his desires in preference to God's revealed
will and walks in love seeking to glorify God in all he does.

It is the process of bringing a young man to full maturity, equipped for every good work and challenge that God will sovereignly place before him.

Not all men have fathers who are believers. My father (Leo) did not come to Christ until he was nearly 50 years old. I never knew my grandfather (Jacob) because my father had run away from home when he was a teenager. Reading through family genealogies I have discovered that my grandfather was a Christian, a member of a Baptist Church and most likely a lay pastor at one time. Jacob, no doubt, had prayed for his "prodigal son", Leo. His prayer was to be answered as his grandson (me) preached to his son (Leo) the Good News of the Kingdom. While Leo was lying sick in a hospital bed, Jacob's grandson, David, would pray with Leo as the prodigal gave his life to Jesus Christ. I can just imagine Jacob in the heavenly places seated with Christ, rejoicing with the angels when his son repented and came to Christ. Leo was no longer a lost son but a joint heir and fellow partaker in the Kingdom of God.

Though our earthly fathers may not have been men who modeled the grace of God, they were still well within the sovereign plan of God. When we realize that God is absolutely sovereign, our thinking and feeling move to a new plane. We begin to loosen our grip from earthly, man-centered thinking to viewing life from an eternal plane. This then is one of the essential ingredients to be a disciple. **We must learn to see things from God's perspective.** That is one reason why it is so important to never become bored with the Bible. Within it's pages the mind of God is revealed to us so that we may sufficiently grasp a view of life from heavenly places.

Because all of life and history is centered in the cross of Christ, **we must be mindful of the purpose and work of the cross** continually. This is another essential element of being a disciple. Some of Jesus' disciples had been with John the Baptist. Some had grown up in the religious Jewish community. But all had incomplete knowledge of who God was, His will and His ways. Nicodemus said to Jesus, "How can these things be . . . ?" (John 3:9) Jesus answered him, "Are you a teacher of Israel, and do not understand these things?" Just as the teachers of Israel, John's disciples and

Christ's disciples also, we need guidance (discipleship) to help us to grow in knowledge and understanding of the Holy One.

What does a pastor do? My quick answer is, *"He leads, he feeds and he protects."* A pastor is a guide to the body of Christ. God laments through the prophets of the Old Testament that the pastors had become corrupt. The role of the pastor, as alluded to in Psalm 23, is to lead the sheep into green pastures and beside still waters. As pastors we must look after the flock with all due diligence. Discipleship is the means of doing this.

My calling for the last 15 years has been to be a pastor to pastors. By guiding young men in Mexico into a better understanding of walking with God, I have found that my influence extents to the churches as well. Taking time for the training of disciples as Christ did will extend your influence far beyond what you may imagine. Keep in mind, though, that it is not our influence, which we seek to expand. It is the influence of God the Holy Spirit bringing glory to God the Father through Jesus Christ, which we strive to carry to nations across the globe. You may not be thinking of an international ministry. I hope you are thinking of the sheep in your care first of all. Be faithful in the small things and let God lead you to the bigger things. Being faithful where He has placed us is often the doorway to the next assignment that He has prepared us for.

As I have followed God's leading from one assignment to another, God has brought shepherds into my life for guidance. Some have been sent to me and guide my development, while others have been there to aid and encourage me. Each successive group of shepherds has been more obedient to God than the previous. They have been more loving, wiser, more experienced and more fruitful than the previous ones. It seems as if God continually orchestrates ever-widening opportunities to be part of what He is doing on this earth.

Testing is an essential ingredient of discipleship also. Each of these men that I have known has been tested in such a way as to cause them to demonstrate their faithfulness. Proverbs 20:6 says, "Many a man proclaims his loyalty, but who can find a faithful man." Testing is a part of life. Many men may proclaim their fidelity but testing will prove it. The test of obedience to every word of God reveals whom a man fears. A man either fears men or he fears God; the behavior that proceeds from a test demonstrates whom he fears.

Many will work for the praise of men rather than the praise of God. *When a man succumbs to pleasing men it is because he fears men. If he obeys the Word of God even when it hurts to do so, he fears God.* This sort of uncompromising endurance reveals the man of God and separates him from men of the world. Many desire to do the work of "the ministry" for the benefits that it will bring them. They may not be paid well but they may live for the respect of men. They may see the role of leader in the church as a route to respect, meaning and purpose. In time this man will stumble and fall away or produce division or trouble the church.

Our high calling is to let Jesus Christ live through us. His high calling was to reveal to men the glory of God in Himself by living as He did and dying as He did. His resurrection and ours with Him are the source of our success. Our death with Him and our resurrection with Him hold the message of the Gospel in bodily form. His cross must be our cross. When we seek to please men we are worried about reputation. When we seek to please God we are worried about nothing but His glory. Nothing else is important. Men pleasers seek out methods to expand the kingdom, or should I say to expand "their kingdom". Methods have their purpose for a season, but godliness with contentment leads to greater and more lasting gain for the kingdom of God.

Christ's method was men. He poured Himself into men. He loved them, lived with them, walked with them and talked with them. The "ministry" isn't some thing we do but rather something that we are. It is not a job, but a life of pouring ourselves into others just as Christ did. This attitude will reap a true kingdom reward.

In America I am looked upon as a poor man. In other nations I am looked upon as a rich man. Either is incorrect when riches are defined by coins, counting or clamor. I am rich beyond my imagination because I have tasted the riches of the goodness and mercy of God. These are riches that satisfy! Those that understand this are truly wealthy! I have tasted this through the presence of the Holy Spirit, through the men who have loved and guided me, and through the churches that have demonstrated the love and compassion of God.

Method makes the difference between whether we become mechanical or marvelous. A man trusting in the latest method will soon become boring, rather than shining as a beacon. Some ministers grow through encouragement, while others out of frustration become enraged. This list could go on and on, but as we are tested God refines us. Those who do God's will in God's way become purer and purer. Those who are purified become powerful messengers. Frustration isn't a hindrance to their ministry.

Yet those who, after testing and trials or the discipling hand of God, resist His cleansing and cling to their own methods will eventually fall by the wayside.

Many a promising leader starts out well and appears to be anointed by God, but upon being tested reverts to trusting in his own charisma rather than humbling himself and submitting to God. It is not unusual that until a man is older and has been through the refiner's furnace many times that he is recognized as a true man of God. Even then many of his contemporaries may fail to recognize the hand of God because of their own failure to permit the refining process to complete itself. The anointing that a man tested by God possesses is the hand of God upon him. James calls it, "the crown of life". (James 1:12) There is an extraordinary sense about him that people are either attracted to or repelled from. It is the very nature of God exuding from his heart. Rivers of Living Water flow from him. (John 7:38) The Spirit of God is free to so flow from this man so that people are convicted of their sin and sense their guilt when they are even near him. They are drawn by the love of God to Jesus Christ. These are the men we seek to be and to develop in the discipleship process, men after God's own heart, men who love God more than life itself. These are the sort of men we are called to be. ***This is the goal of discipleship. This type of man brings glory to God.***

Two of the disciples were walking along the road to Emmaus talking with another whom they did not recognize. (Luke 29:13-35) When they finally realized who it was that had been with them, they said, "Did not our hearts burn within us while he was speaking . . . ?" From time to time I have heard a preacher whose words penetrated my heart so deeply and so profoundly that it would be hard to describe the experience. I have made a feeble attempt at describing it as, "A cool breeze blowing right through me, convicting, cleansing, and comforting my soul." It is unmistakably the touch of God. It is the unmistakable Spirit of God penetrating the division of my soul and spirit and convicting me of sin, revealing His will, while comforting and cleansing me as only God can do. The ability to discern the difference between a good preacher and the man who speaks for God will develop as you grow spiritually.

Do you have a favorite Bible character or hero of the faith from Scripture? Mine is Enoch. We know little about him, but we know enough. "Enoch walked with God . . ." (Genesis 5:24) This is a good man to follow.

I may seem to have gone on and on with this first letter but I enjoy sharing my heart with you. The time we spent together at the conference in Iowa caused our hearts to be knit much like David and Jonathan. It is my desire that the letters that you receive will be of sincere blessing to you, to your family and to the brothers in Ghana. May God richly bless you above what you are able to ask and think!

Lord Bless,
Pastor Dave

Letters To Prince Paul Volume 1

Discussion Questions

Chapter 1—Discipleship: Becoming God's Man.

1. What are some of the goals of discipleship mentioned in this chapter? How are these goals being accomplished in your life?
2. When Pastor Dave refers to "the cross as being the central theme of history", what do you understand that to mean? What are some of the implications of this?
3. How does one "pour himself in others"? Give some examples.
4. What are some of the things we can learn from the life of Christ about how to pour ourselves into others?
5. Can you think of examples from your own life when you were tested and demonstrated either a "fear of God" or a "fear of man"? Be ready to share an experience.
6. Anointing? What is it? How important is it?
7. How do you need to change to assure that God is getting the glory and not you?

The Second Letter to Prince Paul

Pride: It is NOT all about you!

The Issue of Pride

Dear Prince Paul,

I hope this letter finds you again basking in the glory of God, each day more amazed than the last with His goodness and mercy.

In my first letter I expressed my thoughts on the goal of discipleship. I hope that they were clear and an encouragement to you.

When I came to Christ I was not a good reader or a good student. Studying the Bible helped me to learn vocabulary and to read more. I would place a dictionary beside my Bible and look up words that I did not understand. When commentaries were given to me they were even harder to read, and again the dictionary was an invaluable tool. Possessing a thorough grasp of language(s) helps us to more vividly expound the scripture. Language is a tool that God has given us to deliver His message to men. Having the flexibility and understanding of when to use it correctly is our task as messengers. Ambassadors from your country are well versed in language skills and persuasiveness. We as ambassadors of the Kingdom of Heaven are wise to be developing these same skills.

In the Americas, we use the terms "blue collar" and "white collar" to describe laborers versus office workers, respectively. Being a boy from the farm I feel very blue collar, but having the education of a doctor I am also identified with white collar workers. Among Christ's disciples we find both the laborer and the office worker. Fishermen are hard working men. A tax collector may have been an educated accountant. Paul was both an educated theologian and a laborer often working to pay his way in life. Paul understood his humble estate. His time in prison most assuredly helped him to stay humble, as did the thorn in the flesh (2 Corinthians 12:7) that God gave to Paul to keep him focused on the sufficiency of Jesus Christ.

I say all this to remind you to never forget where you come from. Most men have humble beginnings. We work to gain educational and experiential advantage to "add value" to our lives. Most Christians also find, that no matter what we do to "add value" to our lives, returning to our humble roots is where we see God produce the greatest fruit. The chronology goes like this: We are born humbly, we strive to improve our condition, God humbles us and we become more satisfied and fruitful than ever.

There are many themes and lessons throughout the Scriptures that are repeated over and over. ***One such theme is that of humility and pride.*** Pride existed before creation. It was the sin that caused Lucifer to be thrown down from heaven along with one third of the angels. (Isaiah 14) It is such an infectious disease, that it is easily transferred to a naïve host and then willfully sustained. The condition is pandemic to the human race.

Pride takes hold, thrives and justifies itself whenever I look for prestige for my self instead of being 100% totally and completely satisfied with the sufficiency of Jesus Christ. Though we are complete in Christ we sometimes fail to trust in Him completely. We too often are driven by our emotions, which are easily corrupted. Putting faith in my position in Christ is the cure to pride and self-aggrandizement. Few men have been trained to understand and apply ***the doctrine of our position in Christ*** in a practical way. ***This is another essential of discipleship***. Today's letter will touch on the folly of pride and its fruit. In subsequent letters I will discuss the doctrine of our position in Christ and how this doctrine is foundational to all growth and maturity.

Pride takes hold and justifies itself whenever I look for prestige for myself outside of Jesus Christ. A young pastor in Mexico used to ask me how his sermon was after each Sunday service. This went on for nearly six weeks. I gave him the same answer each week: I would say to him, "Did you study the Scripture thoroughly and use it carefully in your message?" "Did you do it in the power of the Holy Spirit rather than in your own strength?" "Did you avoid promoting a personal agenda or expressing personal opinion, but instead remain true to God's message in the Scripture?" Each Sunday he would say yes to these questions and I would then reply, "Then it doesn't matter what I think about how you did as long as the Spirit of God was free to do His work in the hearts of men." ***It is not about us. It is about the glory of God.***

The favorite tool of Satan is pride. In the Garden of Eden, Satan used his favorite tool when he told Eve she would "be like God". (Genesis 3:5) He addressed her emotions and circumvented her spirit. He dealt with her on the level of the soul and awakened a desire that she perceived was unmet, even though she lived in a perfect state. She accepted pride's bait and the rest is history.

David, "a man after God's own heart", walked humbly before God as a shepherd. He trusted God alone when he lived in the fields with the sheep. His source of strength and wisdom were his dependence upon God. Later as he ran for his life from Saul for more than ten years he continued to acknowledge his total submission to the Sovereign One. Yet after he had been used as a tool in the hand of God to bring glory and honor to God as king, he forgot his humble estate. Rather than being satisfied in the Lord, he sought to satisfy himself outside the will of God. He took another man's wife and satisfied his body with the degrading sin of adultery. Again, the rest of the story is history.

Over and over we see the pervasive sin of pride at the root of the ruin of men's lives. It was the primary cause of the hardening of the heart of the Pharaoh. It was the prime cause of the hardness of the hearts of the Pharisees, "the teachers of Israel", which eventually led them to them to seek a way to murder God in the person of Jesus Christ. Unrepentant pride leads to hardness, and hardness leads to extreme forms of sinful behavior. Romans Chapter One maps this out well.

Pride is ugly! It leads to the demise of everyone it infects! Its treatment is: acknowledgment and repentance, and its antidote is humility.

One of the difficult experiences that we have faced as missionaries in Mexico has been watching men disqualify themselves from ministry due to pride. The scenario shared by missionaries is similar throughout developing nations. (It is not that much different in developed nations.) In developing nations there seems to be a wide gap between the haves and the have nots, or the rich and powerful and the poor and powerless. Money and power go hand in hand everywhere. When a movement of God touches a group of people there is a need for leaders. Among developing nations, schoolteachers and university professors grow into a sort of middle class. They are admired, and due to their higher standing economically and socially, develop a middle class that becomes decidedly influential. What does this have to do with the church and pride? Leaders naturally are needed in the church. These leaders fill roles as pastor-teachers. Do you see the association? When a man becomes a teacher or leader in the church he can easily feel as if he has risen to a level above his peers. In many developing nations the model of leadership is one of suppressing the masses and lording it over the poor. Knowing no other example, the new pastor can easily copy the leadership model of society rather than that of Scripture. He in essence puts himself in the place of God to his flock. Rather than speaking for God he can easily usurp the role of the Holy Spirit. The priesthood of the believer is sacrificed, and fear of man replaces the fear of the Lord. It is a subtle deviation but the results are destructive to the leader as well as to the movement. Authority must be maintained in the church, but this authority is derived from fidelity to the Word of God and not to positions.

In 1st Timothy chapter 3 we are admonished not to place a novice in the position of an elder/pastor/overseer/bishop. (Each of these is an interchangeable title.) This is a universal warning to all cultures. Be very careful not to award such a high position to an untested man. A man must have proven character. Many young men will practice a behavior of respectability in front of "men of position". They do "all the right things" with the hope of being rewarded for their good behavior. This type of person has missed the point of true Christian leadership. *We are all slaves and bondservants.* We do not wield the authority of men, but the authority of God. This authority is not reached by position or power, but by the influence of acts of love through servanthood. Ours is not a human kingdom where position can be attained by strength or cunning manipulation. Over and over I have seen men tested. Some have had a pure heart to guide them, and have chosen to obey scripture no matter what the cost. Still others, when tested, revealed the impurity of their heart and did what was expedient, though contrary to Scripture, to maintain or advance their position. *When lust for power has taken root in the heart, tragedy follows.*

God appoints as he anoints. We must be aware of His appointments. Then we must obey God no matter what. *Our success is manifest in our obedience to God in acts of love toward people.* The novice or fleshly man, as evidence of "success", often interprets a position or title as proof of his worthiness. But success in the kingdom comes with submission and obedience to every word of God, seeking God's glory and not our own.

Proverbs says a "man is tested by the praise accorded to him". (Proverbs 21:27b) When I am hungry for praise, I am close to stumbling and falling. When we receive praise, how does it settle within us? When I am anxious for praise what is at the root of this desire? Is my first thought, "Thank you lord that people are seeing you glorified"? Or deep down inside am I frustrated and angry when someone else gets praised before me, including God? Do I long for "first place" among the brethren? Are Christ's words, "The greatest in the kingdom must be least of all" a rebuke instead of a pleasure to my ears?

Have I (or we) invited God to do whatever it takes to make me (or us) the person He wants me (or us) to be? Or have I put limits on what God is allowed to do with me? Have I ever thought, "God mold me, but don't make me look bad." I have watched as tribes' people from southern Mexico walked the streets of larger Mexican cities on trash-pick-up-day going through thrash barrels seeking food for their families. I have asked myself, "Am I too proud to eat from trash cans?" The day may come for this sort of test. These are defining moments in our lives. Do I honestly admit my condition or try to bury the truth about my pride? Pride can be "buried" beneath hundreds of layers of the sediment of justification or repression, but its roots are hardy and surely will rise to the surface of one's life. Unless the axe of repentance cuts the root of pride early, we will live to regret that we did not deal with it when God gave us the chance. The humble man will learn a lesson from these unexpected moments when the heart is laid bare. In these moments we decide our future. Proverbs says, "He who conceals his transgression will not prosper, but he who confesses and forsakes it will find good." (Proverbs 28:13)

A proud man cannot realize success within the Kingdom of God. He can only become frustrated and move closer to the discipline of God or hardening of his own heart.

Pride seeks position, but bond-slaves take joy in sacrifice for the benefit of others.

Tests along the road of life are opportunities to conceal or confess our sins.

"Pride goes before destruction and haughtiness before stumbling." (Proverbs 16:18)

"How blessed is the man who fears always, but he who hardens his heart will fall into calamity." (Proverbs 28:14)

Be very careful. As men who are looked up to by others, we are in a temptable position. Satan has slung his fiery missiles of pride in our direction many times. When he speaks to leaders he says things in first person like this: "This movement needs me." Or, "This is my church." Or, "They depend upon me." **God, not us, causes kingdom growth.** We are tools that he uses. He uses us so that He may be glorified, and we may be amazed by His mercy. He invites us to participate in His work so that our joy may be full. When we sacrifice it is because He has changed our heart and given us the desire to do so. When we choose to do what is right even when it hurts, these actions tell us how much He has taken control of our lives. He makes us like Himself.

When we are humble we counter the lies of Satan with the truth. When we are proud we tend to accept these lies and justify them. We need to tell Satan, ourselves, and our friends this sort of thing: "God alone has done this thing! This movement is a miracle of God! We are but tools in our Master's hands being used as He sees fit that He might be glorified."

Our prayer should constantly be, "Please, Lord, keep me in a state of constant brokenness and humility. Search me, O God, and try my heart. Know me and expose my faults and lead me in the paths of your righteousness." (Adapted from Psalm 139) "Lord you are the Potter and I am the clay. You have the right, and my permission, to do whatever you desire with me."

What a Way to Live! Bondservants of the Greatest Servant!

Lord Bless,
Pastor Dave

Letters To Prince Paul Volume 1

Discussion Questions

Chapter 2—Pride: It is NOT all about you!

1. Has God provided an experience for you that has been helpful in maintaining humility? Be ready to share that experience.
2. Can you identify a "thorn", some sort of problem that God has given to you to help in maintaining humility? Be prepared to share this also.
3. What do you see as possible ways to look for prestige in and out of the church?
4. In what ways do you think pride manifests itself?
5. Can you remember a time when you have justified some misbehavior because you were afraid of what people would think? Then what did they think?
6. Are you hungry for praise? Are you curious of what people think about you? If so, why do you think this is? Discuss this thoroughly.
7. Do you fear God or do you fear men?

Third Letter to Prince Paul

The Gospel: Simple and Complex

Dear Prince Paul,

Writing to you has turned out to be a pleasant challenge, helping me to focus on the things of God in an orderly manner.

The last letter I sent to you seemed to take a long time to write. The issue of pride is so huge that I feel that we only touched upon it. It is important to remember that it is the primary stumbling block of mankind. Pride quenches the Spirit of God. Pride also keeps our minds from the illumination of the Holy Spirit to the Scriptures. In your life you will have many opportunities to see the result of its work. Later in life you may look back and see how pride played a role in your own life and see how God has changed you as He has faithfully molded and shaped you along the way.

I promised to talk to you about our position in Christ. We will get there soon. Today we will begin a discussion of the gospel. Knowledge of our position in Christ is where all spiritual life and health emanates from. But first let us begin with a discussion of the gospel.

I've heard pastors and teachers ask people many times if they could explain the gospel. Simply put, the gospel is the good news that "Christ died for our sins". (1Corithians 15:3) Off course, we must add that He rose from the dead. (1Corithinas 15:4) Then there is the need to explain that we must respond when we hear it. Without repentance and belief there is no appropriation. (Acts 3:19) With each sentence there is more information, and with more knowledge the explanation grows. The gospel is simple but, in addition, with a growing intimacy with God it becomes expansive. Growing in Christ leads to an expanded understanding of the gospel. As a result we can make it too complex for the first time listener.

It should be presented in a simple fashion to sinners outside of Christ, in order that the Holy Spirit may illumine their minds, convict them of sin, righteousness and judgment, and draw them to Christ. (John 16:8)

In subsequent letters we will discuss the value of an expanding knowledge of the Gospel but at this point I want to make an application that is important. A question asked by leaders of all movements of God is, "How do we keep this movement alive? How do we sustain this awakening?" First of all, *it is God who causes and keeps any movement alive.* But secondly, we must consider causes that lead to quenching of the Spirit's activity among us. While many are coming to Christ, we don't think about the future of the movement but are excited about what is happening in the present. In our emotional state we can overlook insidious stumbling blocks along the way. God is blessing and we are thrilled. But even in the early stages of awakening, we would be wise to learn from past lessons in the history of other movements.

A good example of a movement of God getting off track and becoming something other than God intended can be seen in the to churches that grew out of methodistic preaching of circuit riders of the 19th century in western frontier of America. I grew up in one these churches that recently had their 100th anniversary. Methodism began as a movement of God through the preaching of the gospel by Charles Wesley. His sermons were clear and simple, and many of his disciples copied these sermons and preached them also. This repetitive style or method subsequently became known as Methodism. Originally Methodism preached Christ. But as the years went by they lived on the past success of their simple methods and did not move on to full maturity. Looking for meaning, they redefined their purpose and became a social reform movement. They lost their focus on the gospel and are now a declining church worried about membership, unaware of their departure from God's purposes. This can happen to any great movement of God if the leaders are not careful to keep the purpose of God in view.

That aside it is important to learn lessons from history. One such lesson is *the lesson of preaching either the "simple gospel" or the "complex gospel"*. We know that the gospel is both simple and complex. Earlier I described the simple gospel. Can it be simplified even further than that? Can it be reduced to a word? What one word would sum up all that is contained in the gospel? The answer is . . . The gospel cannot be summed up in word but it can be summed up in a person . . . Christ. Christ is the gospel.

But the gospel is also very complex. When we consider the complexities of who God is, how can it be simple? When we examine all that Christ accomplished and each of the doctrines that grows from His finished work on the cross, we see that there is much to understand.

Here lies the paradox that often confuses us. The gospel is simple and at the same time complex. As a church develops it must strike a balance between the focusing on the simple and on the complex. Many churches come into being when the simple gospel is preached and God opens people's hearts. These events are a marvelous work of God. They are so marvelous to us that we do not want to depart from the sense of awe we have experienced in our new life in Christ. We shouldn't. At this point we are newborn babes in Christ and grow as children do spiritually. As the change physically from children to adults comes about, dietary needs change, and more complete or complex foods are necessary for growth. The same is true spiritually. To grow in grace and knowledge of the Lord Jesus Christ, a healthy spiritual diet must be provided.

As we pass from stage to stage in our spiritual development it is easy to resist change. Since we felt secure in each prior stage, we can be hesitant when asked to move on. Often churches, having been thrilled by the joy of the simple gospel, are afraid to move on to more maturity. After all, it was the simple gospel that accomplished such marvelous changes in our lives, so why would we want to forsake it? The answer is, "We never should." But sometimes a church or movement can get stuck there and not move on to full maturity. Paul writes about this in Hebrews 5:12-14. Though these believers should by this time have been mature teachers themselves, they were still acting as babes in Christ. Our protection of the pure and simple gospel can in reality be overprotection. It can stunt our spiritual growth and thus quench the Spirit and the power driving the movement.

We must grow in knowledge and grace. Focusing on simple grace alone will not help us to grow in all ways in Christ Jesus. You have probably seen an adult acting like a child. They may be 30 years old but act like a 10 year old. They are adult children. Their growth and development has been arrested emotionally. They are not stable or responsible. Their behavior does not match their stature.

The same thing can happen to an individual, a church, or an organization. They can have the appearance of being full-grown but inside they are immature. A church body can have existed for a long time, but its behaviors might not demonstrate the maturity that we see in Christ. This may come from poor feeding, poor modeling, but is often caused by a diet of the "simple gospel" only. This could be called an "evangelism only" church. They are stuck in the evangelism mode. Sunday messages meant to feed the flock are just another hour of sharing the simple gospel message. (That sounds negative but there is an explanation coming.) This church may also have become nostalgic and preoccupied with reminiscing or trying to recreate the "good old days".

What stops the work of God? Quenching the Spirit can stop Him from working in our midst. If God appears to have ceased working, we should consider what we have done to quench the Spirit. There has to be some form of disobedience to which this can be traced.

Just as a church can get stuck in evangelism mode only, it can also run the risk of getting stuck in a "teaching" mode. As people see the need for understanding God better, they begin to read the Bible, study it and listen to more preaching. The epistles become a source of an explosion of knowledge at this stage and they begin to taste of the depths of the riches found in Christ Jesus. But the danger here is that they become so enamored with this fresh, and new and exciting stage of growth that they forget evangelism and the simple gospel.

When we are fed and full we become dull. We become comfortable and are safe in the new fortress of knowledge. But fortresses were meant to keep people out. They are designed to be defensive edifices. They are not conducive to mounting an attack on the gates of hell. How are we going to storm the gates of hell, if we have become dull and comfortable in our fortresses? What a tragedy when a movement of God degenerates into a system of self-protection! Some would say that it is not long until this movement is over.

Is there a cure? Can a movement gone dull be revived? Can we keep this from happening? Like most things in our spiritual lives the cure is the same. Repentance is called for. We must examine our lives, identify disobedience and repent. We must turn back to Gods' ways, and away from ours. A mature Christian is not one who knows more. *A mature man of God is one who sees his sins and does not make excuses for them.* He sees his sin and quickly admits it. A mature Christian is a "*rapid repenter*"!

So what have we seen thus far? The gospel is simple and it can be summed up in a word, "Christ". But Christ is unfathomable, and therefore the gospel is also complex. *The simple and the complex should live side by side.* Concentrating on either one by itself places any church in a weakened position. But giving both their balanced place is a Biblical position. We must commit our efforts to doing the work of an evangelist, while at the same time teaching the complexities of doctrine. Combined they serve to strengthen the church and assure its continued fruitfulness. If I evangelize with the simple gospel and do the hard work of studying and expounding the Scripture, there will be health and life in my church. To do anything less leaves the church in a weakened position. The healthy position is to maintain a balance between the two. We must never cease to plant and water the Seed and wait for God to bring the harvest. At the same time we must be teaching the doctrines of the Scripture to our flock so they may be healthy and be able to give an answer of the hope that is within them. (1 Peter 3:15)

Healthy people grow and reproduce. Healthy churches grow and reproduce. Healthy believers reproduce healthy new believers. Healthy churches give birth to more healthy churches.

Churches that sow bountifully reap bountifully. Churches that sow sparingly also reap sparingly. Churches that feed the flock for the purpose of equipping them to minister are full of good fruit. Feed the flock to fatten them, and they are only good for being led to slaughter.

Do not lose your zeal for sowing. Paul said to Timothy, "Do the work of an evangelist". (2 Timothy 4:5) "Stir up the gift of God that is within you." (1Timothy 4:14) Don't be too simple or too complex, but build a balanced ministry plan that encourages your people to grow in the *grace* and the *knowledge* of the Lord Jesus Christ. Maintain that balance, obey every word of God, confess and forsake sin, be a "***rapid repenter***" and teach others to do likewise. These together will go a long way toward seeing the movement of God in your midst continue to flourish.

Until Next Time,

Lord Bless,
Pastor Dave

Letters To Prince Paul Volume 1

Discussion Questions

Chapter 3—The Gospel: Simple and Complex

1. What does the author mean by the simple and the complex gospel?
2. What was your reaction to the statement, "Christ is the Gospel"? What are some of the implications of this?
3. Can you think of an example that you have witnessed of resisting change and growth? Can you share a time when you have resisted healthy change?
4. How would you characterize your understanding and practice of maintaining a balanced ministry?
5. What is your "reproduction" track record? Both personally in regard to making disciples and corporately in regard to starting new churches, how are you doing?

Letter Four to Prince Paul

Our Identity: Walking in the Spirit

Dear Prince Paul,

I recently took some time to make a mission trip into Mexico to visit churches and do some leadership training with visiting ministers from the United States. That is the reason for the lapse in writing to you. I also found that I had not healed quite as much as I had hoped from my stroke, and that the trip was more strenuous that I had supposed it would be. Now I feel quite rested and ready to resume our communications. How many times have I said that?

I had promised to write to you about the importance of understanding our position in Christ. This is a central doctrine to the Christian life. This doctrine is summarized in Galatians 2:20 which states, "I have been crucified with Christ, but it is not I who live, but Christ lives in me and the life which I now live, I live by faith in the Son of God who loved me and gave Himself for me." Memorizing this verse and meditating upon it will be important over the rest of your life.

The principle of our position in Christ, or our identity in Christ, is the subject that I teach on more than any other topic. Even when it is not the primary subject, its principles are woven into most of my teachings. It is essential for us to understand this doctrine if we are to walk by the Spirit. *We are to do all that we do from our position and new identity in Christ.*

Here is a verse that is often quoted. II Corinthians 5:17 says, "If any man be in Christ he is a new creation; old things have passed away, behold all things have become new." I would read and memorize that verse as a young believer, and always "feel" as if I was not grasping it fully. I was not until I had been a Christian for about seven years that I began to understand enough doctrine to begin to more fully appreciate the reality of my new life in Christ. By the end of my first decade as a Christian and on into the second, my understanding of being "in Christ" began to take root.

Moving on in our growth, we begin to think in a manner that expands our faith. It is true that we ask Jesus to come into our hearts, and we think in terms of "Christ in us the Hope of glory". (Colossians 1:27) It is true that Christ has come into our lives and sealed us for eternity. (Ephesians 1:13, 4:30) These are glorious truths. We think about these verses as new believers because we are capable of easily grasping these concepts. We understand things from our limited perspective. But scripture reveals an unlimited God. When we think of Christ in us, we are considering the goodness of God within us. That is a wonderful thing to be grasped.

It is also true that we are "in Christ". Christ is in us, but we also are in Christ. This is a subtle but profound difference of perspective. This moves the focus away from us, and puts the emphasis on Christ. Our perspective and thinking is stretched as we consider much more. As we think of being in Christ, we begin to see a larger view of God.

Preachers often remind us, "When God looks at us He sees Jesus Christ and not our sinfulness". That's true. But another way to view the same truth would put it this way: *"God looks at His Son, Jesus Christ, and finds us in Him."* The emphasis is now on Christ more so than on us. My thinking moves from a focus on self, to who Christ is and what God sees in Christ. God sees the perfection of the second person of the Trinity. God sees the obedient God-man, emptied of Him through death on the cross. God sees us in Christ, crucified with Him. When we look at ourselves as God sees Jesus, we are able to view ourselves with a whole new identity. This gives greater meaning to what I wrote earlier when I stated, "It's not about us; it's all about Jesus."

Many people have taught this perspective throughout the history of the Christian church. This form of thought seems to be downplayed in times when the church has declined. When we look at ingredients of long lasting awakenings, we see the Christian's position in Christ being a prominent teaching. Here are some of the teachers that have placed an emphasis on our identity in Christ. Men like Augustine in the first century, later reformers like Martin Luther and John Calvin, and more recent preachers such as Charles Spurgeon, Lewis Sperry Chaper, Martin Lloyd Jones, Charles Stanley and John McArthur remind us of the importance of our position in Christ. The book, "Hudson Taylor's Spiritual Secret" is a chronology of his discovery of the importance of understanding our position in Christ. This then is *another "essential of discipleship"*.

My pastor of 17 years, Rev. Dick Weins, would say, "the good often robs us from the best". He would go on to say that living for Jesus is good, but letting Jesus live through us was best. Understanding our position in Christ and our co-crucifixion with Him aids us in considering ourselves dead to sin and alive to Christ. Jesus living through us, what a way to live! When we live "for" Jesus we are focused on how "self" can be of use to God. When we consider ourselves dead to sin and alive to Christ, He expresses His life, His will and His desires through our faculties. The issue of understanding the self-life's competitive nature to the Spirit-life is vital to our spiritual lives. In Galatians 5:16-25 we read much about walking according to the Spirit and not according to the flesh.

At this point I want you to consider that the "works of the flesh" aren't just vile sins that are easy to point out in "bad" people. The flesh is prominent in all of us. The essence of sin is living a proud self-centered life. Like Eve in the garden, we have a "better idea" on how and who is to meet our needs. Any time I try to meet my needs for love and acceptance outside of Christ, I am living a self-focused life. I am walking by the flesh. Some men want to be pastors so that they will be respected. That is fleshly thinking and behavior. Position in this life will not fulfill me. Only Christ can completely satisfy. Men everywhere are deceived by position, power or possessions. None of these can fill the void that plagues all of us. But men pursue all sorts of means, including religious ones, to meet their needs.

This is the point at which many need to stop and take a breath. We ask ourselves, "Isn't living for Christ a good thing?" Remember that the good often keeps us from the best. More than anything, the world needs to see Jesus Christ incarnate, in us. The principal of being "dead to self" is at the core of a life that glorifies God. A man who says "not my will, but yours dear Father" has considered himself dead to sin and his desires. Considering God's will above our desires, vision, and aspirations flows from considering ourselves dead to sin. Living in our identity in Christ gives Him the freedom to empower our minds to see His purpose for our lives. The Southern Baptist Pastor, Henry Blackaby says this, "Asking, 'What is God's will for my life?', is the wrong question". Asking God what His will is for your neighbor, or your community or your country is the right question to ask. Then you will know what His will is for you. When we know God's will for those around us, we can drop our plans and join God in His stratagem. Do you see how this takes the emphasis off of us (self) and moves it to God? It is not our will but His that matters. Dying to self is a matter of surrendering my will and letting God's will take its place.

This is the essential path to being filled with the Spirit. Many talk about the filling of the Holy Spirit without obedience. Many talk of the filling of the Spirit without discussing surrender and death to self. The path to experiencing Christ living through us is one of coming to the end of our resources and submitting our will to God's will.

In my next letter we will spend time considering this issue further. It will take several letters to expound on our identity in Christ. Focusing on our identity in Christ will lead to a new and healthier perspective on walking by the Spirit.

Lord Bless,
Pastor Dave

Letters To Prince Paul Volume 1

Discussion Questions

Chapter 4—Our Identity: Walking in the Spirit

1. Have you memorized Galatians 2:20?
2. How easily or how often do we find ourselves focused on ourselves instead of being focused on Christ?
3. Compare and contrast thinking of "Christ in us" versus being "in Christ".
4. Can you think of some possible reasons why when the church is in decline that the idea of being "in Christ" is downplayed?
5. Since the flesh is very prominent in all of us, how do you see yourself competing with the Spirit of God? How do you need to repent?
6. Are you surrendered to God's will and free from your own will?

Fifth Letter to Prince Paul

Brokenness: The Work of the Holy Spirit

Dear Prince Paul,

Before beginning this letter, please open your Bible and read John 12:20-32.

Several years ago I spoke for the closing of a missionary conference using these verses as my text. The topic was on the importance of brokenness on the part of every believer.

In this letter we will talk about what the Word of God does and more on the importance of death to self, which can also be described as brokenness. A great book can be downloaded from the Internet that covers this subject. If you do a search for "The Calvary Road" by Roy Hession, you will find many complete online copies. "The Calvary Road" may be my most recommended book. It is a must read for all believers and describes the need for brokenness and humility better than anything else that I have read.

Isaiah 55:11 is an important verse to understand. In it we hear God say to us, "So will My word be that goes forth from my mouth; it will not return to me empty, without accomplishing what I desire, and without succeeding in the matter for which I sent it." John 16:8 states, "And He (the Holy Spirit), when He comes will convict the world concerning sin and righteousness and judgment."

What the Word of God does when expounded in the power of the Holy Spirit is to expose men to their core beliefs, their true nature, their real motivations, the horrid character of their inner man, and the filthiness of their flesh. Simply put, it convicts them of their sin.

As the unbeliever goes about life, being able to avoid hearing God's Word, he is happy that he has not been exposed to his wretchedness. *It is a terrible thing to know how sinful a man I really am. It is both terrible and good; for without it I would never know of my need for Christ.* When the unbeliever hears the Word of God for the first time the result is that the Word cuts deep into his heart and exposes his sinful condition. As it is laid bare a person instantly reacts. Reactions vary widely, but there are basically two types of reaction to conviction of sin, wrongdoing and guilt. You may have seen many manifestations and types of behavior when people come under the judgment of the Holy Spirit, but they can be looked in two ways. The two reactions that occur are:

1. **A person is drawn to God.** (or)
2. **A person is repelled from God.**

Does that sound simplistic or does it make sense? I believe that one or the other of these happens each time we preach the Word of God and each time we hear the Word of God. In the early stage of an awakening, and in areas where new churches are developing, we see people drawn to God through the preaching of the Word, repenting of their sin and making professions of faith in Christ. Let me remind you that it's not our preaching that causes this; it's the Holy Spirit that is doing this great life-giving work. He has just chosen to use the preaching of the Word to be the means of delivery of His work of drawing men to God. Think of yourself as a "delivery boy". You have probably also seen those who do not respond and who may even get defensive or become reactive.

These two types of responses are not limited to evangelism and salvation experiences. As we grow in Christ, we do so because of exposure to the Word of God followed by obedience to what we hear. Being drawn to or repelled from God happens at every significant stage of our spiritual growth or regression, respectively. Obedience leads to growth and disobedience leads to regression.

I have seen leaders rise to positions of importance through apparent commitment and faithfulness. I have also seen some of these same leaders, after hearing an important message from Scripture, begin to fall away from God and great was their fall. The "higher" we rise; the farther we have to fall when we react to conviction without repentance and obedience. If our motivation has emanated from the desire for the praise of man, and the Spirit of God exposes this to us, we must repent immediately. If a person does not respond to God immediately in repentance then he will quench or grieve the Holy Spirit. What follows is a long silence while God waits for our obedience. During this period of quenching or grieving the Holy Spirit there is a troubling void of silence, as we do not hear the voice of God. This may take place even though we listen to much preaching. When we listen to preaching in this state we are troubled, but not by the Spirit of God. We are troubled by our guilt. A struggle ensues within the heart. Fruit begins to disappear from our lives, and we increase our efforts to appear fruitful but with great distress. Deep inside we know what God wants us to repent of. Yet if we do not repent, then we must repress the knowledge of how God has asked us to change. This repression of the truth makes us even more barren and we become spiritually sickened. As others are enjoying their spiritual riches around us, we become dry, and soon become secretly angry. Our countenance and demeanor begin to change from lack of joy. Jealousy of others fruitfulness begins to rule over our mind. Can you see the downward trend? Repentance must be the way of life for a growing Christian. Failure to say yes to God is disastrous. A mature Christian is a person who repents rapidly; he is a "rapid repenter".

One type of brokenness comes from the Spirit of God. Another comes from rebellion toward God. When the Holy Spirit judges us and we respond in brokenness, repentance and obedience, we have experienced a brokenness that is pleasing to God and indescribably wonderful for us. The presence of God is more real at this time than any other, and this sort of brokenness becomes a place that we desire to abide continuously. It should be, because this is the place that Christ desires for us. This is where He abode during His earthly residence.

The other type of brokenness comes from the consequences of sin, rebellion, lack of repentance and doing things our way. Living without God leads to broken lives. By the world's standards, some will have terribly broken lives that reflect the circumstances of their lifestyle or culture. Some will have fairly successful lives with a portion of difficulty that varies. Others will have pleasant circumstances that many envy. These are all relative and consider life from an earthly or physical perspective. It is easy to avoid considering what man was really made for. *We were created to glorify God and enjoy Him forever.* Without a relationship with Christ even the most pleasant life is a broken one. This may describe the man who has not met Christ and also the one who has come into close contact with Him but instead of repentance has imitated the Christian life with religious flesh. I think religious flesh that has grown out of disobedience to God leads to the worst sort of brokenness.

Psychologists talk about a mechanism natural to all men that we use to deal with stress. It is called the *"fight or flight"* mechanism. When faced with a stressful situation, (like conviction), we either fight the source of the stress or we flee this same source. Being a natural response, we see the natural man or the fleshly man consistently use these. Therefore, when an unrepentant person is faced with sin or wrongdoing, they will either fight the source of the conviction or flee. What if you are the source? What if you have preached the Word of God and a person does not want to respond in obedience to the conviction brought upon them by the Holy Spirit? What if this has been the case for some time and this person has been trying to hide his disobedience with religious behavior (religious flesh)? The principal of "fight or flight" still applies. A person living by natural resources (self), and not by Christ's resources, will either attack the messenger or avoid the messenger. If we pursue the brother who is avoiding us, wanting to help him toward correction and he does not want to repent, he will have to switch to the fight mode and attack us with lies or slander or even worse. (This how the Pharisees dealt with Christ.) I have experienced this many times. I have thought that a brother would be happy to correct a behavior that is not Biblical, and when I pursued this matter the person turned against me. It is a very sad scenario but reality from time to time. You will surely experience this, if you have not already.

The flesh is always with us, and we must be aware that it is a cruel antagonist of everything that the Spirit of God desires for us. The only cure is death, ***death to self***. We must examine our lives and become aware of every pattern that we have used prior to becoming a Christian and some that have been modeled for us after coming to Christ. Each of these flesh patterns must be recognized and rejected. Ask yourself over and over, "What is my pattern of walking after the flesh? Do I use flight or fight in reaction to stress or conviction?" All of us do one or the other, or both, and need to let the Spirit of God rule our lives so that our behavior is marked by His fruit; His love, His joy, His peace, His patience, His kindness, His goodness, His faithfulness, His gentleness and His self control. (Galatians 5:22) When we are filled with the Holy Spirit the fight or flight mechanism is not an option. Love and obedience are the supernatural first choices.

Christ died to set us free from our sins. It can also be stated that he died to set us free from our flesh and ourselves. Paul said, "For me to live is

Christ . . ." (Philippians 1:21a) He had learned of the contentment that is found in the sufficiency of Jesus Christ rather than his own insufficiency.

This is a struggle that we all must pay attention to. Christ was tempted in all ways as we are. (Hebrews 4:15) We can see in John 12:24 that Christ had just shared how a grain of wheat must fall to the ground and die. He was referring to His own death and how we must also follow Him. Then in verse 27 he expresses how troubled He is. In Christ's humanity He experienced every difficulty that we do. He later said, "Not my will, but thy will be done." (Matthew 26:39) We will wrestle with our will, our flesh and our desires but as long as we maintain a repentant and broken lifestyle, it will be our pleasure to choose to do God's will, even in the face of much difficulty.

When I refer to the flesh I am referring to us getting our needs met outside of Christ. The sufficiency of Christ is an important subject on which to meditate. 2 Peter 1:3 tells us "He has given us everything pertaining to life and godliness". And in Colossians 2:10 again, "In Him we have been made complete". Focusing on our identity in Christ and our completeness in Christ will help to maintain our fellowship with Christ and our walk by the Spirit of God.

In the next letter we will look at Romans chapter 6 and consider the instruction God has provided for us to walk by faith in our new identity in Christ.

I pray that you continue to walk by faith and set your heart and mind on Christ to fulfill the calling that God has assigned to you. With your mind set on Christ, your calling will be fulfilled with the same joy as was set before Him. His joy will be your joy.

What a way to live!!!

Lord Bless,
Pastor Dave

Letters To Prince Paul Volume 1

Discussion Questions

Chapter 5—Brokenness: The Work of the Holy Spirit

1. What was your first reaction to the conviction of the Holy Spirit?
2. Do you have an experience that you feel free to share when you resisted obedience and repentance? How did God work with you during this time?
3. Are there safeguards that we can build into our lives to help us to avoid disobedience, and lack of repentance which results in a downward spiral spiritually?
4. What is your flesh pattern, fight or flight, and how does it manifest itself in your behavior?
5. How can each of us encourage one another to walk by the Spirit?

Sixth Letter to Prince Paul

Dead to Sin: Crucified with Christ

Dear Prince Paul,

Joni and I deeply grieved to hear of your illness and have asked many here to pray for you. Our desire is that you continue to glorify God through it all.

The brothers who have been reading and reviewing these letters have given good feedback. Knowing that you are the primary recipient of these letters, they are also praying that you are encouraged, edified and empowered to pass on sound doctrine to the men you serve.

It is always good to write out your thoughts and messages. Until we began this project I relied upon an outline as a guide and memory tool for both teaching and preaching. Someone has said that reading gives you more knowledge; speaking helps you communicate better and writing works to make you more precise.

Today we'll begin to look at Romans Chapter Six verses 1-14. Please take some time to read these verses or have someone read them to you. These are good verses to memorize.

This section of scripture starts out by asking a question that someone had raised about behavior of believers. The question had arisen, "If we live by faith then why are our actions or behaviors of any importance?" Our actions are of great importance for a number of reasons. First of all, we represent God and therefore our actions should be as holy as His actions. 1 Peter 1:16 tells us to "be holy, just as I am holy." Another obvious answer is that Christ died to free us from our sins, not to free us to sin. Salvation by faith is not a license to live as we wish. Christ's death set us free from our sin. His resurrection life, which has been so graciously placed within us, empowers us to obey His Word, do His will, walk with Him and be his body in this present age. His death sets us free from bondage to sin, and His resurrection gives us the life we need in order to be people who are now free to glorify God in these bodies.

In verse 2 of chapter six Paul says, "How shall we who died to sin still live in it?" *One of the great facts of salvation is that we have died to sin.* Here we are introduced to the teaching of our co-crucifixion with Jesus Christ. We will discuss our co-crucifixion, or co-death, as well as our co-resurrection with Him. Recall Galatians 2:20 where Paul states, "I have been crucified with Christ . . ."

Verse three of chapter six goes on to remind us "Or do you not know that all who have been baptized into Christ have been baptized into His death?" (We'll assume here that we are not talking about our water baptism, but about our baptism by the Holy Spirit of God, which seals us in Christ at the moment of salvation.) How were we baptized into Christ's death? We have to begin thinking in terms of our new spiritual condition and not in terms of an earthly, human perspective. We are spiritual people now and must begin to understand spiritual realities. Before we came to Christ our spirits were dead to God and alive to sin. We lived totally in the sphere of the physical and soulical (personality). Now that our spirits are made alive in Christ we must use our personality (our mind in particular) to consider what has taken place.

It is wise at this point to describe the tri-fold makeup of a man. In 1Thesselonians 5:23 we see this stated, "may your spirit and your soul and body be preserved complete."

The body is the **physical** suit that each of us wears to be able to survive in the confines of this earth. Just like a fireman wears a fire suit, a businessman wears a business suit, or an astronaut wears a spacesuit, so we wear this physical body as an earth suit. Adam and Eve were given physical bodies that have been passed down genetically to every human being.

The second part of a person is the **soul**. This is where we really live. You see the expression of the person inside, through the body. The real me is inside. The real me uses the body to communicate with the rest of the world. The soul can also be called the personality. *The soul or personality has three parts also. These three parts are the mind, the emotions and the will.* You could also call these the thinker, feeler and chooser respectively. It is the mind of the believer that goes through the process of renewal. Romans 12:2 talks of being transformed by the renewing of our mind. This is a gradual process carried out over the lifetime of a believer as he fills his life with the Word of God and walks in obedience to all he learns from it. Through the exercise of the will (the chooser), we decide to fill our minds with God's Word and either obey or disobey. Obedience brings the blessing of illumination to our minds and a filling of the soul by the Holy Spirit. You will, at times, hear preaching that seems mechanical even though it is truthful. Sometimes you will hear an emotionally expressive man preaching the Word of God, but in your heart you will have a sense of questioning. You will also have the wonderful experience of sitting under the influence of truly godly men and your "heart will burn within you". (Luke 24:32) The difference comes from the preacher's source. He is either drawing from the soul (self) or from the spirit (the Holy Spirit). One preacher preaches for reputation while the other preaches for the glory of God. Both share the Word of God and the Word is powerful, but the later preacher's message is empowered more so by the Holy Spirit. This is a result of the humility brought on by obedience to every Word of God. When Christ spoke to two disciples on the Emmaus road they couldn't help but experience this, for Christ had been obedient even unto death. Many preach with less than pure motives and even Paul was happy that they did, so long as Christ was preached. (Philippians 1:15) But there is nothing that compares to the Gospel being preached for the right reason in the power of the Holy Spirit.

A quick mention needs to be made about *emotions*. God made them. They are wonderful but as fallen people we must be careful not to let emotions rule our lives. Emotions are meant to help us experience the joy of the Lord and the joy of life when we are in proper relationship to God and others. Emotions should follow obedience to truth. Emotions should not determine the course of life. We should learn this from the example of Adam and Eve in the garden. They were deceived by a lie and the emotions that moved them were untrustworthy. Our emotions are wonderful, if they are the fruit of healthy spiritual lives.

The mind, the will, and the emotions are the three parts of the soul. We live and express what goes on in this area of our being every day. Having a healthy spiritual life depends on a good understanding of the soul.

The third part of man is the most important. It is the spirit of man. This is the part of man that relates to God. When Adam and Eve sinned, they died. But after they sinned they kept on walking and talking. They hid, they expressed fear and they were embarrassed. Then how is it that they died? The prominent part of their lives, the spirit, died. Their bodies did not die. Their souls did not die. But their spirit died to God and came alive to sin. When the scripture says that we are dead in our trespasses and sins, this is the part of us that is being referred to. The most important part of us, our spirit, died. The central part of our being was destroyed by sin. This sin separates us from God. We no longer have a means to relate to God because our spirit is dead to God and alive to sin. Only in regeneration, a work that only God can do, is our spirit made alive and our ability to have a relationship with God restored. The common biblical term for the dead spirit is the natural man, the old man or the old nature. The spirit of man determines the nature of man.

When Adam and Eve were created the spirit ruled their lives. They had no guilt, no fear, and no embarrassment. They walked around naked in the garden with no thought of their natural state. Their spirits, which relate to God, were prominent and their souls and bodies were subordinate. The order of importance was spirit, then soul, then body. *The result of the fall of man into sin has reversed this order.* Why is so much importance placed upon how we look or feel, instead of on our spiritual needs? This is the result of the fall. As long as Adam and Eve continued to walk in obedience to God their bodies and souls enjoyed physical, mental, emotional, and spiritual health. When Satan came to Eve he used deceit, leading to emotional manipulation, to draw her into his diabolical plot. In the garden Satan subtly sowed the seed of doubt and mistrust. Eve was caught, and the rest is history.

Let's tie this together with Romans 6. *It is in the realm of the spirit that regeneration takes place.* It was the spirit of man that died in the garden. A void was not left. The spirit did not disappear, but instead became alive to sin. *The spirit influences the soul directly.* Adam and Eve immediately became aware that they were naked. They hid and became afraid. At the instant of their sin they became aware of good and evil and their natural state.

After the fall, the core of man was a nature alive to sin and dead to God. Now, when a man repents of his sin and believes in the work of Christ upon the cross, a miracle takes place within him. That sinful nature, natural man or old nature (however you want label it), our sinful spirit that was alive to sin is counted as nailed to the cross. This is our co-crucifixion. Christ bore our sin in His body on the cross. This gives much greater meaning to Paul's commentary in Galatians 2:20, "I have been crucified with Christ, nevertheless, it is not I who lives, but Christ lives in me . . ." *Being "crucified with Christ" is not just a figurative statement, it is the reality of every believer and is accepted by faith.* We have died to sin through the obedient work of Christ on the cross in the same manner as Adam and Eve died to God through one act of disobedience. (Romans 5:19) We have died and our lives are hidden in Christ. (Colossians 3:3)

It is a great truth that Christ died for sinners. It is equally important that know that our sins were nailed to the cross. We died with Christ. Therefore, no matter how we feel (be careful of those emotions), or what we have or have not been taught, we as believers have died to sin. We live by faith and not by feelings. God is not a liar. What He says to be true is true. ***Faith, is believing that what God says to be true, is true.*** Living by faith is a wondrous adventure. My salvation belongs to Christ. My life belongs to Christ. It is what He has done that counts for everything. Now I can consider myself dead to sin and alive to Christ. He is my life. Martin Luther said, "Christ became all that I am so that I might become all that He is."

A lot happened at the cross. The sin of every believer fell upon Christ. The load was astronomical.

As a side note let me say this. It is not an accident that both contaminated water and venomous snakebite have made you sick nearly to the point of death. I am not surprised that such a dreadful condition has come upon you. Brokenness, like you are going through, is a common experience for all who choose to walk fully in obedience to Christ. All godly, obedient men throughout history have suffered to a significant degree in relationship to their calling. Even the hand of Satan is used to bring about greater knowledge of God. (Job 1) Paul's list of troubles reminds of this also. (2 Corinthians 11:24-33) It is after we have been brought lower than we can bear and have no other resources that we experientially understand Christ as our only source of life. We may say that we understand this but not nearly as well as we do after the breaking process. (See all of Job) Paul said "For me to live is Christ and to die is gain." (Philippians 1:21)

These are great moments of growth in your life. It is God who is at work in you to do His will and good pleasure. (Philippians 2:13) These will be days that you look back on with fond memories of how God took you through great testing and brought you out purer than you could have ever dreamed.

We'll continue to discuss Romans 6 in our next letter.

From One Broken Servant to Another,

Lord Bless,
Pastor Dave

Letters To Prince Paul Volume 1

Discussion Questions

Chapter 6—Dead to Sin: Crucified With Christ

1. As you consider the three-part makeup of man can you come up with a diagram that helps to illustrate this?
2. Can you also diagram the three parts of the soul? Think of ways to label these parts to help you remember their roles.
3. Discuss how the three parts of the soul interact and integrate with each other.
4. Discuss how you have witnessed the makeup of man turned upside down. How do you see the physical and soulical taking precedence over the spiritual?
5. What things can we you do to return the role of the spiritual to its proper place of importance?
6. What parts of the Scripture are opening up to your thinking and what should you do to exercise your faith as a result?

Seventh Letter to Prince Paul

Alive Again: Resurrected to Life in Christ

Dear Prince Paul,

It was good to hear that your health has returned and that you see this as a gift from God to serve on in His sovereign will. I sent a note to all whom I have trusted to pray for you, and I am confident that they too are rejoicing with you.

You may wonder why I say, "People I trust to pray." Many people say that they will pray but experience tells me that not all do. Some say that they will, and some will. It is my pleasure to have identified persons who I can trust to pray.

In our last letter we began to look at Romans 6:1-14. Let's continue to look into these verses. Take some time to read them again.

Remember in our last correspondence how we considered the reality of every believer's death with Christ. We call this our co-crucifixion. Our sin has been nailed to the cross with Christ. He bore our sins at Calvary. What a great truth to behold! Christ who knew no sin became sin for us. (2 Corinthians 5:21)

Chapter six, verse four goes on to tell us that we have been buried with Christ. Not only was the sinful core of our being nailed to the cross, but also it was buried, as all dead men need to be buried. So when Christ rose from the dead a new life rises with Him. The old man is dead and buried and we are raised in newness of life with Christ. With Christ's life in us we are able to walk in this newness of life.

Before, in our unbelieving state, our spirit was alive to sin and dead to God. As we discussed in our last letter, this is the part of man that was crucified and buried. As a result we are free from the tyranny of our sinful nature. We are no longer slaves to sin. Our sinful nature was crucified and buried. Now we live with new life within us. We have experienced a co-death and burial with Jesus Christ.

We also now experience our co-resurrection as we are raised with Him in His resurrection. We have His resurrection life within us. He did not resurrect our old man but crucified it and has given us His very own resurrection life in the person of the Holy Spirit. He resurrected a new man, Himself. That is the life that now works in us and makes us spiritually alive. Observe verse six where it tells us, "Knowing this, that our old man was crucified with Him, that our body of sin might be done away with, that we should no longer be slaves to sin." We are free! We are free from sin!

These are facts stated clearly throughout the New Testament. These are facts that our faith must rest in. Remember that ***faith is believing that what God says to be true, is true***. I am dead and my life is hidden in Christ. (Colossians 3:3) Keeping this in mind will help to bring our lives into focus.

Also remember, we live in the area of our personality (soul). Each of us has thoughts and emotions that are prominent. One person may be more objective (thinking and fact oriented), while another may be more subjective (emotion and feeling oriented). Both types of people need to grow in faith. The objective person has the advantage of trusting facts. His "facts" may be wrong but at least he is engaging his mind first. The emotional person needs to discipline himself to engage the intellect, as he becomes a student of the Bible. As each places his trust in the truth (facts) of the Scripture, his mind begins to be filled with the kind of information that will cleanse and renew him. Changes in both thinking and emotions should naturally follow. The highly objective person will soon find himself "feeling" loved and accepted, and emotions that might have been dormant are awakened. Joy floods his soul. The subjective person soon begins to engage his mind more and more and puts less and less confidence in how he feels about things. Instead, he puts his emotions to the test of the truth of the Scriptures. The Word of God begins to rule his heart and the truth of God rules his life. What may have felt natural at one time now becomes a warning sign to him as he pays closer attention to reason and truth.

Psychologists and counselors teach a model that they have observed in human behavior. It is called the TFA model. We can see that it is not something they invented, but something they have observed, since God has already placed this in mans behavior. The "T" stands for *thinking* or the mind. The "F" stands for *feelings* or emotions. The "A" stands for *actions* or the will. Recall in our last letter how we defined the divisions of the soul. Here we see counselors observing what God has already fashioned within man.

This is what they have observed:

T-A-F (Thinking - Acting - Feeling)

The person who THINKS first, and then ACTS on those thoughts, has healthy FEELINGS about himself. Since this man's behavior is well thought out and his decisions are based on things he has been taught, his mental and emotional health is very good. The emotions of this man are very much in control and are a healthy asset.

F-A-T (Feeling - Acting - Thinking)

The person who is motivated by his FEELINGS, and then ACTS on them without much THOUGHT has consequences to consider for a long time. His emotionally driven behavior leads to impulsive decisions and actions. This person's emotional condition vacillates. His moods swing from very happy to very sad. He has placed confidence in his emotions because they are what make him feel good. (He often denies the bad.)

A-F-T (Act - Feel - Think)

People who have operated in the FAT mode very long may move toward this. They Act without thinking. Parents often think that our children are like this much of the time. In reality, the AFT mode is just a rapid FAT process.

The preferred style of behavior is the TAF mode. People who haven't yet disciplined themselves, been disciplined by others or have not been trained and disciplined by God will do whatever has been easiest all their lives. That is why Romans 12:1-2 is so important in the process of spiritual growth.

Romans 12:1-2 says, "Therefore I urge you, brethren, by the mercies of God, to present your bodies a living and holy sacrifice, acceptable to God, which is your spiritual service of worship. And do not be conformed to this world, but be transformed by the renewing of your mind, so that you may prove what the will of God is, that which is good and acceptable and perfect."

Presenting ourselves a living sacrifice brings us back to submitting our lives to the will of God rather than to our will. We must sacrifice our selfish and worldly desires and follow the will and desires of God. We can sacrifice our will when we are considering ourselves dead to sin and its selfish lusts, while simultaneously obeying God. This is the act of dying to self and living according to who we now are in Christ. Understanding the will of God and the ways of God are part of the process we go through as we grow in Christ. The process must include the gradual transforming of our thinking, our feeling and our resulting actions. Note the emphasis in Romans twelve verse 2 on the renewing of our minds. We see here that ***the transformation in our lives is accomplished primarily at the level of our mind***. As an act of the will we must put ourselves in a position where we learn more and more about the Scripture so as to know more about God, His will and His ways. Preaching, teaching, fellowship and discipleship around the Word of God are the primary means of accomplishing this.

Though our minds may have been filled with the Word of God, we do not automatically become godly. We must obey. ***Obedience is the key.*** Many a man has been filled with the Word but the fruit of his life does not show that he has been transformed. Renewing of the mind takes place after we have been filled with the Word of God while having a submissive heart. As this takes place throughout our lives, there is a transformation seen by us internally, and by others externally. Another result takes place as we obey God. The Holy Spirit fills us (empowers us) and gives us illumination to scripture, wisdom, spiritual sensitivity, discernment, love, joy, etc.

The religious leaders of Christ's day were experts in the Law but their lives did not demonstrate spiritual vitality. They lived by the letter of the Law and not by the Spirit of the Law. Jesus called them "whitewashed tombs". They looked good on the outside but were rotten inside. Because they did not have a heart to obey, they fell away. It is easy to become just like these religious leaders. If we do not focus on His will, we focus on ours. Ours is self centered, egotistic, and self-serving. We will seek glory for ourselves if we do not consider ourselves dead to sin and alive to God.

One of the old catechisms says, "The chief end of man is to glorify God and enjoy Him forever." ***God can only be glorified when self is out of the way***. Death to self gets it out of the way. That is why it is so important to focus on our position in Christ. We can only live according to who we are in Christ when we consider ourselves dead to sin and alive to God.

If you will recall, I defined the filling of the Holy Spirit in one of the previous letters. More than any power, we need the power of the Holy Spirit flowing through us in everything we do. Whether we are playing with our children, or speaking to a large group of people, we need the Holy Spirit to fill us and flow through us. God designed us to live in fellowship with Him. This is accomplished when He lives through us. ***We can't have fellowship with Christ, without Christ.*** And only Jesus can live the Christ life, the Christian life. It is through complete submission to God that we experience the life of Christ living through us. ***God has never asked us to improve ourselves to better relate to Him.*** His solution is death. He died for us. He died in our place. He died and took our sins upon Himself. He was crucified for us. AND - ***We were also crucified with Him, buried and raised up in newness of life with Him!*** This is what makes the Christian life possible. It is Christ's life. It is not about us, it is all about Jesus Christ.

As we THINK this way, it follows that we should ACT accordingly (walk in obedience). The Holy Spirit fills our souls and then we feel the love and joy and goodness of God as never before. (There's the TAF model lived out in our spiritual lives.) His love, His mercy and all that is true about Him are manifest because it is He that is living through us, manifesting Himself in us.

I have one more letter to write in this series. Since the topic that we have been covering is our position in Christ, co-crucifixion and co-resurrection we should be sure to examine this in other scriptures. One principle of hermeneutics is that a doctrine should not be developed from just one verse, one location in scripture, or one book of the Bible. As you read your Bible you will begin to see the believers co-crucifixion and co-resurrection in many places throughout the New Testament. You will also begin to see places in the Old Testament that will begin to unfold more clearly with this in mind. In our next letter we will especially focus on passages from Ephesians and Colossians. You might want to read ahead and look for these passages.

Our adventure in Christ is a great one. Some people say that the church exists to win people to Christ. That is just a byproduct of the Christ Life. When we walk in our new identity in Jesus Christ, what will we want to do? You are right! We will want to tell people about our relationship with Jesus Christ and invite them to join us in this same wonderful adventure of knowing Christ. Evangelism and spiritual growth naturally flow from Christ. Christ drew people to Himself when He was incarnate. He still does this through His body when we are dead to self and alive to Him.

What a way to live!

Lord Bless,
Pastor Dave

Letters To Prince Paul Volume 1

Discussion Questions

Chapter 7—Resurrected to Life in Christ

1. Please describe in your own words what each of the following mean: co-crucifixion, co-burial, and co-resurrection.
2. What habits do I have in place to facilitate the renewing of my mind? Discuss this as a group and begin to practice a new habit to begin to practice.
3. How closely do you relate to each of the TFA models?
4. What are some ways that we can encourage and help each other to walk in Christ?

Eighth Letter to Prince Paul

Faith to Faith: It IS all About HIM

Dear Prince Paul,

I hope that you have been reading ahead in Colossians and Ephesians and have come across the verses that I alluded to in my last letter.

The first series of verses is in Ephesians chapter two. The entire chapter should be considered as a complete thought. It has some great things to say about our position in Christ and the resulting realities that will manifest in our lives as we focus on Christ as our life.

If you have been around the modern church very long you have no doubt heard Ephesians 2:8,9 quoted endlessly. They are great verses and help people to understand that it is not works that save us. Do you recall letter three in which we discussed the simple gospel? If not, go back and review that letter again. When the simple gospel is shared, these are two verses that are often used and it is important to do so. But, how did the original readers hear these verses? They were heard in the context of the entire letter to the Ephesians, and specifically in the thoughts expressed in chapter two.

The modern church has slipped away from study of biblical doctrine. We are prone to pull a verse or pair of verses out of a page of scripture and use them as proof texts for a position. Many of these positions are good but, with the isolation of verses as proof texts, we also isolate our thoughts from the purpose of that particular text. Ephesians 2:8,9 do tell us that salvation is by faith and not by works but because they have been used so widely just for that purpose, our minds move more toward thoughts of evangelism than the author's original intent. Looking for the author's original intent will go a long way towards opening our eyes to greater breadth of knowledge of God. It will help to move us from simple, but naïve faith, to a profound grasp of the endless riches of Christ laid out for us in the pages of the Scripture.

This chapter is a prime example. Verses 8 & 9 are a continuation of the expression of the immensity and beauty of the work of the reconciliation process accomplished in Christ. Verses 1- 9 lay out this process with great clarity in a developing order that leads to our grasp of fellowship with Christ. We are His workmanship from beginning to end.

Romans 1:17 tells us that in the gospel "the righteousness of God is revealed from faith to faith . . ." Why do you think that Paul uses the word faith twice in this sentence? (From faith to faith.) I believe it demonstrates Paul's stress upon faith. We are born into the kingdom of God by faith in the finished work of Christ. All He accomplished at the cross also sustains us in the kingdom. This too, we accept by faith. We appropriate maturity (sanctification) by trust (faith) in His work as well. In other words, we are saved by faith and sanctified by faith. His righteousness is revealed in us from faith to faith.

The point of focusing so much time on our position and identity in Christ is to get us to truly walk by faith. It is to get us to trust in Him to work through us rather than us "doing great things for him". The later arouses pride but the former ushers in humility and brings glory to God. We are not saved by faith so that we can grow by our best personal efforts. Our best personal efforts could not save us. How can we imagine that they will have any value toward sanctifying us? We come to life by faith, and we walk in Christ by faith. Too often we preach salvation by faith and then preach about sustaining life by personal effort (law). We want our people to live holy lives, but too often use guilt preaching to get them to change. It is a work of Christ in the heart that leads to lasting change. Teaching people to walk by faith, according to who they are in Christ, brings about internal transformation followed by external evidence. We cannot produce evidence of change among our people and should not try to. This is a work of the Holy Spirit, which He accomplishes in the inner man. It is only aided by us to the extent that we model a walk by faith and teach others to do so also. (Be wary of manipulating people's behavior with guilt. We learn this from our mothers, not from God.) Paul says, "The love of Christ controls us." (2Corithians 5:14) There is a type of church that motivates by guilt, and there is a type of church that encourages the believer to walk by faith. I believe that God prefers the latter.

Paul wrote the entire letter to the Galatians to counter the notion of self-sanctification. Among the Galatians there were those who were teaching the necessity of returning to laws and traditions to be "true" Christians. Galatians 3:1-3 contains some piercing statements: "(1) You foolish Galatians, who has bewitched you . . . ? (3) Are you so foolish? Having begun by the Spirit, are you now being perfected by the flesh?"

Why is it so easy to acknowledge salvation by faith but then be so proud of our own efforts to grow? We answered this question in letter number two! It is the problem of pride. *We love our salvation by faith, and we love our self-righteousness. The two cannot live in the same house.* Eventually God will expose the futility of our self-effort, and as conviction and repentance follow, we will surrender to Christ alone. We say salvation is through Christ plus nothing. The same is true for sanctification. Spiritual growth comes through surrender and submission to Christ and abandonment of self-effort.

The natural argument that follows is, "Do I do nothing?" No! You do not do nothing! You obey! You surrender, submit and obey His will. One surrenders to an enemy. Once we were enemies with God. Self-will and God's will are in opposition to each other. I surrender my self-will and submit to God. Even if my will was to preach the gospel, I must surrender it. God knows my heart and motives and what is best for the kingdom and I may need to live in last place for the remainder of my natural life to glorify Him. It is only after living there that my preaching is of real value to the listeners that God sets before me.

Ephesians 2:10 states, "We are His workmanship, created in Christ Jesus for good works, which God has prepared beforehand so that we would walk in them." The works of service that we do are His idea, not ours. We must be continually in an attitude of surrender to Him so that we are able to recognize what these works are those He has prepared for us to do. We learn this from Jesus' example. He did nothing except for what the Father had shown Him do. (John 10:37, John 14:10) I may be able to think of many things that I want to do for God, but these can easily displace me from what God wants to do through me. We must abide in Him (John 15:4) in surrender and fellowship and see what those works are that He has prepared beforehand. When we participate in those works, there we bear the kind of fruit that only God could produce. When we make our own plans, there is human fruit, which eventually spoils.

I want to touch briefly on Colossians today also. Colossians 3:1-3 states: "(1) Therefore if you have been raised up with Christ, keep seeking the things above, where Christ is, seated at the right hand of God. (2) Set your mind on the things above, not on the things that are on earth. (3) For you have died and your life is hidden with Christ in God." Verse three sums it up. We have died and our lives are hidden in Christ. Setting our minds on Christ will set our feet to walking in the right direction. This entire chapter is rich with instruction on walking by faith in our true identity in Jesus Christ.

There is always more that can be said, but sometimes more is not more. More can become too much and confuse the issue. I am satisfied that I have covered the essentials of the beginnings of understanding our identity in Christ with you. My son-in-law is planning to put these eight letters on line so anyone that would like to do so can read them. Anyone will be free to download these letters from the Internet. When they have been proof read and all the spelling and punctuation has been corrected, they will become available.

I have been thinking about the form of the church as it is laid out in the Scripture and the form of the church as we see it operation today. The shape that it has taken in the past century, and how frustrated believers are in experiencing all that God intends for them in fellowship with Him and one another, has driven me to prayer. James 1:5 instructs us, "But if any of you lacks wisdom, let him ask of God, who gives to all generously and without reproach, and it will be given to him." I have sought God's wisdom in this matter for several years and I believe He has answered this prayer through a number of sources. The answer to this question has come a piece at a time and seems to have all come together in the past few months. If you are willing, I would like to share this with you next. It would be my pleasure to write another series of the "Letters to Prince Paul" concerning the form of the church as seen in the first century while also considering how the modern missiological church can benefit.

It has been my pleasure to share these eight letters with you. May God give you wisdom and understanding far above what you are able to ask and think!

Lord Bless,
Pastor Dave

Letters To Prince Paul Volume 1

Discussion Questions

Chapter 8—Faith to Faith: It Is all About HIM

1. The proper study of Scripture should follow rules of exegesis. Have you heard of these rules for study? Can you put together a practical list for yourself?
2. How is it that the author can say, "Just as we are saved by faith we are also sanctified by faith?"
3. In what ways can we be more careful on how we preach to be sure it is not us trying to elicit change in people but rather trusting to the Holy Spirit to be the agent of change?
4. Is "self-sanctification" a new term to you? Please discuss this term.
5. Throughout the book the theme of humility and pride have been common threads. In what way(s) have you become more aware of this important issue in your life?
6. As an individual and preferably as a group, are you beginning to identify the "good works that He has prepared beforehand to walk in"?